THE URBANA FREE LIBRARY

3 1230 00788 6555

W9-AXD-459

DISCARD
URBANA FREE LIBRARY

2—12

DATE DUE		
MAR 27 2012	APR 0 9 2012	
JUN 0 4 2012	JUL 0 5 2012	

The Urbana Free Library

To renew: call 217-367-4057
or go to "*urbanafreelibrary.org*"
and select "Renew/Request Items"

Dear Parent:

Congratulations! Your child is taking the first steps on an exciting journey. The destination? Independent reading!

STEP INTO READING® will help your child get there. The program offers five steps to reading success. Each step includes fun stories and colorful art. There are also Step into Reading Sticker Books, Step into Reading Math Readers, Step into Reading Phonics Readers, Step into Reading Write-In Readers, and Step into Reading Phonics Boxed Sets—a complete literacy program with something to interest every child.

Learning to Read, Step by Step!

Ready to Read   Preschool–Kindergarten
• big type and easy words • rhyme and rhythm • picture clues
For children who know the alphabet and are eager to begin reading.

Reading with Help   Preschool–Grade 1
• basic vocabulary • short sentences • simple stories
For children who recognize familiar words and sound out new words with help.

Reading on Your Own   Grades 1–3
• engaging characters • easy-to-follow plots • popular topics
For children who are ready to read on their own.

Reading Paragraphs   Grades 2–3
• challenging vocabulary • short paragraphs • exciting stories
For newly independent readers who read simple sentences with confidence.

Ready for Chapters   Grades 2–4
• chapters • longer paragraphs • full-color art
For children who want to take the plunge into chapter books but still like colorful pictures.

STEP INTO READING® is designed to give every child a successful reading experience. The grade levels are only guides. Children can progress through the steps at their own speed, developing confidence in their reading, no matter what their grade.

Remember, a lifetime love of reading starts with a single step!

For Nancy, the lady from Baltimore
—M.K.

For Angie and Jim Denton.
Ad astra per Harley.
—R.W.

Text copyright © 2012 by Monica Kulling
Cover art and interior illustrations copyright © 2012 by Richard Walz

Photo credit: **Armed Forces History Division,** National Museum of American History,
Smithsonian Institution (p. 48)

All rights reserved.
Published in the United States by Random House Children's Books, a division of Random House,
Inc., New York.

Step into Reading, Random House, and the Random House colophon are registered trademarks of
Random House, Inc.

Visit us on the Web!
StepIntoReading.com
randomhouse.com/kids

Educators and librarians, for a variety of teaching tools, visit us at
randomhouse.com/teachers

Library of Congress Cataloging-in-Publication Data
Kulling, Monica.
Francis Scott Key's Star-spangled banner / by Monica Kulling ; illustrated by Richard Walz.
   p. cm. — (Step into reading. A step 3 book)
ISBN 978-0-375-86725-5 (trade) — ISBN 978-0-375-96725-2 (lib. bdg.) —
ISBN 978-0-375-98008-4 (ebook)
1. Baltimore, Battle of, Baltimore, Md., 1814—Juvenile literature. 2. United States—History—War
of 1812—Flags—Juvenile literature. 3. Flags—United States—History—19th century—Juvenile
literature. 4. Key, Francis Scott, 1779–1843—Juvenile literature. 5. Star-spangled banner (Song)—
Juvenile literature. I. Walz, Richard, ill. II. Title.
E356.B2K85 2012
973.5'2—dc23 2011027443

Printed in the United States of America

10 9 8 7 6 5 4 3 2 1

Random House Children's Books supports the First Amendment and celebrates the right to read.

STEP INTO READING®

STEP 3

Francis Scott Key's Star-Spangled Banner

by Monica Kulling

illustrated by Richard Walz

Random House 🏠 New York

Francis Scott Key
loved writing poems.
He wrote them
on horseback.
He wrote them
late at night.

Once Francis
even wrote a poem
after a battle.
It became
America's national anthem.

Francis lived
in Georgetown, Virginia,
near the Potomac River.
He and his wife
had eleven children.

Francis was a lawyer.

People came to him

with their problems.

Francis liked to help.

He was always busy.

Every morning
Francis read the newspapers.
Exciting things
were happening
in young America.

It was now
free of England.
It was free to make
its own laws
and to grow
in its own way.

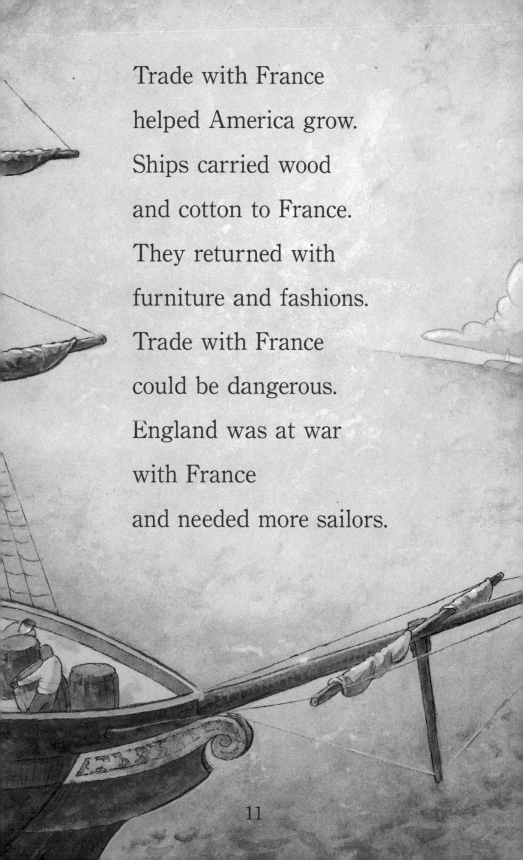

Trade with France
helped America grow.
Ships carried wood
and cotton to France.
They returned with
furniture and fashions.
Trade with France
could be dangerous.
England was at war
with France
and needed more sailors.

British ships followed
American ships
on the high seas.

They took the ships.

They forced the sailors to join
the English navy.

This made Americans angry.

And the anger grew.
America wanted to move
into lands west and north.
But England held forts
in the west.
They ruled Canada
in the north.

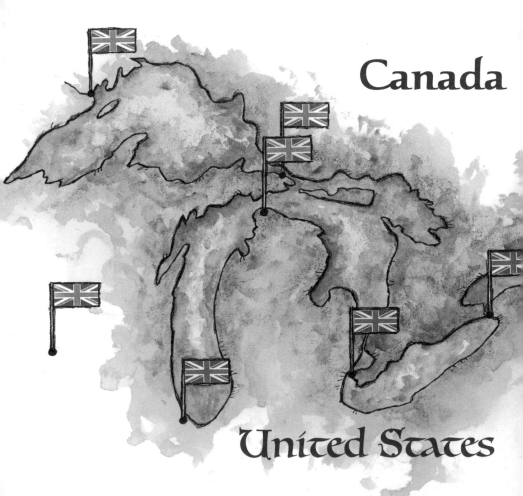

Canada

United States

America would have to fight
England for freedom
to gain new land.
So in 1812
America declared war
on England.

Brirish
Forrs

Francis joined the reserves.
Reserve troops help
regular army troops.
Francis helped the troops
in northern Maryland.
He loaded, fired,
and cleaned cannons.

But he was slow and clumsy.

After ten days,

the army sent him home.

In the spring of 1813,
American troops burned down
government buildings
in Canada's capital.

More than a year later,
the English troops
struck back.

In August 1814,
they marched on Washington.
They set fires
all over the city.
They burned down
the White House!

The British didn't stay
for long.
They planned to attack
Fort McHenry next.
Fort McHenry protected
Baltimore's harbor.

On their march
back to their ships,
the British troops stopped
at Dr. William Beanes's house.
He had helped them before.

But *these* troops
were rude and noisy.
They stole from
the people in town.
Dr. Beanes sent someone
to get American soldiers.

They put the British troops
in jail.
This action made
a British general mad.
General Robert Ross
sent troops
to arrest Dr. Beanes.

The doctor was now
a prisoner of war!
But his friends
knew what to do.

They went to find Francis.

Rap! Rap! Rap!

They banged on his door.

It was late,

but Francis was awake.

"Dr. Beanes is in jail!"

they shouted.

26

The doctor was
Francis's friend.
He wanted to help.

A few days later,
Francis set sail
with John Skinner.
John was a lawyer, too.

Their small ship
flew a white flag.
The white flag was a sign
all sailors knew.
It meant they were coming
in peace.

What if the English
did not care about
their peace flag?
But the English
did not open fire.

The two men safely boarded
the British ship.

Francis had letters
that were written
by English soldiers.
The letters said Dr. Beanes
had helped them
when they were hurt.
General Ross read the letters.
Dr. Beanes would be freed.

But there was a problem.
General Ross would not let
the three men leave.
They knew too much
about the planned attack
on Baltimore.

Francis's ship was tied
to a British ship.

The battle began.

Cannons roared.

Rockets burst.

The air was black with smoke.

"The country is lost
if the fort falls,"
said Dr. Beanes.
"We are safe as long as
our flag still flies,"
said Francis.

The bombing went on
for twenty-five hours!
At dawn all was quiet.
Was the flag still flying?

Francis looked into a spyglass.

There was so much smoke,

he could not see the flag.

He could not even see the fort!

Suddenly sunlight

cut through

the smoke and fog.

Francis saw the flag!

It was flying high

above the fort!

Baltimore was safe.

America was still free.

Francis was filled
with pride and joy.
He sat on a barrel
and began to write
about the battle.

He wrote about how happy
he was to see
the flag still flying.
He wrote about how much
he loved his country.

Francis's poem

was printed in the newspaper.

It was set to music.

Soon people

across the country

were singing it.

We still sing it today

in schools and

at sporting events.

The War of 1812

ended on February 17, 1815.

Francis went back

to his quiet life.

He continued

to help people

and to write poems

until the end of his life.

The commander of Fort McHenry was
George Armistead. America's most famous
flag stayed with his family for almost a
hundred years. Family members cut pieces
from the flag to give to special guests.
They even cut out one of the stars! Today
you can see the flag that inspired the
writing of our national anthem at the
Smithsonian Institution in Washington, D.C.